Celebrity Chefs'
Dish of the Day

Published in 2005 by
New Holland Publishers (UK) Ltd
London • Cape Town • Sydney • Auckland
www.newhollandpublishers.com

Garfield House, 86–88 Edgware Road, London W2 2EA, United Kingdom
80 McKenzie Street, Cape Town 8001, South Africa
14 Aquatic Drive, Frenchs Forest, NSW 2086, Australia
218 Lake Road, Northcote, Auckland, New Zealand

ISBN 1 84537 287 5

Editor: Anne Konopelski
Production: Hazel Kirkman
Design: Alan Marshall
Editorial Direction: Rosemary Wilkinson

10 9 8 7 6 5 4 3 2 1

Reproduction by Pica Digital Pte Ltd, Singapore
Printed and bound by Star Standard, Singapore

Disclaimer
The authors, publishers and British Small Animal Veterinary Association (BSAVA)
have made every effort to ensure that all instructions given in this book are safe and
accurate, but they cannot accept liability for any resulting injuries or loss or damage
to either property or person, whether direct or consequential or however arising.

Celebrity Chefs' Dish of the Day

Over 40 recipes by pet-loving chefs in aid of **Petsavers**

Edited by Mike and Mary Martin

NEW HOLLAND

Contents

Preface

Each day, I am faced with sick pets' anxious owners, who are seeking help and advice. Most times, their pets, with appropriate diagnostic tests and treatments, go on to live full lives. In many cases, research into the diseases suffered by these animals has been funded by Petsavers.

Petsavers was begun as a charity in 1974 by members of the British Small Animal Veterinary Association (BSAVA). These dedicated veterinary surgeons realised that no organisation existed specifically to fund studies into the diseases that affected our pets. Little did they know how successful and far-reaching their fund-raising would be.

To date, Petsavers has given more than £1.7 million to numerous studies and specialist training programmes. These include studies into arthritis and infectious diseases such as parvovirus, and programmes that aim to advance vets' skills in areas ranging from brain disease to cancer. Reassuringly, Petsavers only funds research that involves clinical work. Animals are never used in experiments.

If your own pet has been ill, Petsavers may have funded research into the diagnoses and treatments that were used to manage his or her health. On pages 70–74, you'll find examples of the many animals helped by Petsavers; they could easily belong to you.

You can contribute to Petsavers in a number of ways, all of which are listed on page 76. By purchasing this book, you will also be helping the charity. You will get a flavour of the type of work that Petsavers funds, with the added bonus of having an excellent cookery book full of wonderful recipes.

It remains for me to thank the Petsavers volunteers who worked hard to take this book from conception to publication and those chefs who contributed, realising the value of Petsavers to both their present and future pets.

I hope that Petsavers can look forward to your continuing support.

Carmel T. Mooney MVB MPhil PhD DECVIM-CA MRCVS
President, British Small Animal Veterinary Association (BSAVA)

Acknowledgements

Our thanks go to everyone who has helped to put this book together. All have done so through the kindness of their hearts and with no financial rewards. In particular, we would like to mention the following:

The chefs and their personal assistants

The first chef we contacted was Antony Worrall Thompson. His enthusiasm for the project, as well as that of his personal assistant, Louise, really spurred us on. Antony also volunteered the first recipe and a photograph of himself with his dogs Jessica and Trevor.

Many great recipes were subsequently donated to Petsavers, and our sincere thanks go to all of the chefs who contributed. We also owe a huge thank you to the chefs' tireless personal assistants for their willingness to track down photos and recipes.

We felt that an important part of the book would be the photos of the chefs with their pets, and we were delighted with the response that our request generated. All of the photos are fantastic, and we hope readers enjoy them. Some of the chefs did not have pets at the time of publication but, as K. K. Anand wrote to us, he would love to have a pet – and that thought alone encouraged him to donate two recipes.

Petsavers' staff (BSAVA)

We would like to express our gratitude to the staff at BSAVA headquarters, especially Maggie Berriman and Nicolette Thomas, who work so hard on behalf of Petsavers, and Petsavers chairman Ian Ramsey and the Petsavers Committee, for their encouragement and advice. Thanks are also due to Matthew Poulsin and Graeme Kowalewicz of Fusion Design, for their assistance.

The pets

We have included several photos of pets that have benefited from Petsavers-funded research. Merry, a black Labrador, took part in a project to help to advance imaging techniques used to treat elbow dysplasia. Cardhu, a short-haired domestic cat that developed senility, helped us to better understand age-related brain changes in cats. We hope these images bring you closer to the work that Petsavers supports. We would like to thank the owners for allowing us to use these photos.

You

By purchasing this book, you have helped a worthwhile charity and raised the future level of care that we might give to our pets. If you would like to continue helping Petsavers, please refer to the contact information on pages 75 and 76, or visit the charity's website: www.petsavers.org.uk. Even more importantly, please tell your friends about Petsavers.

All royalties from the sale of this book go directly to Petsavers.

Mary and Mike Martin

Salt and Pepper Prawns

Rick Stein

- Heat a dry wok over a medium heat. Add the salt and stir constantly for about 4 minutes, until it has turned a greyish colour.
- Transfer the salt to a small bowl and mix with the five-spice powder, Sichuan peppercorns and black pepper.
- Pour the sunflower oil into a large pan until it is about one-third full and heat to 180°C/350°F/gas mark 4, or until a small piece of white bread dropped into the oil browns and rises to the surface in 1½ minutes.
- Add half of the prawns and fry for 30 seconds, until they have curled up and turned pink. Remove and repeat with the remaining prawns.
- Reheat the dry wok, add 2 tablespoons of the spiced salt and the cooked prawns, then flip the prawns in the salt for 30 seconds so that it can permeate them. Tip on to warm serving plates and serve the remaining salt separately.

2 tbsp **salt**
1 tsp **Chinese five-spice powder**
1 tsp **ground Sichuan peppercorns**
1 tsp **ground black pepper**
sunflower oil, for deep frying
900 g (2 lb) **raw, unshelled, headless prawns**

Roasted Figs with Goat's Cheese

Anton Edelmann

- First, prepare the cheese filling. Put the goat's cheese and rosemary in the olive oil and leave for at least 3 hours or, better still, overnight.
- Remove the cheese from the oil and pat dry with some kitchen paper. Crumble into a bowl and stir in the double cream. Reserve the rosemary and olive oil.
- To prepare the figs, preheat the oven to 200°C/400°F/gas mark 6. Cut the figs in half, sprinkle with a little sea salt and the orange zest, and top with the cheese mixture.
- Place the figs and rosemary on a baking tray and bake for 6–7 minutes, or until the cheese has melted and is lightly coloured.
- Meanwhile, make the coriander salad. Mix the carrots, spring onions and radishes with the coriander and wild rocket leaves.
- Next, make the beetroot glaze. Reduce the beetroot juice by four-fifths, cool and whisk in the olive oil.
- To serve, whisk the lemon juice with a little of the reserved olive oil and toss the salad in this dressing. Place a fig half on each plate and top with the coriander salad. Pour 50 ml (2 fl oz) of the beetroot glaze over the figs.

Serves 2

175 g (6 oz) **goat's cheese**
1 **rosemary sprig**
150 ml (5 fl oz) **olive oil**
50 ml (2 fl oz) **double cream**
4 **black figs**
sea salt, to taste
zest of ¼ **orange**, finely grated

For the coriander salad:
2 **carrots**, peeled and cut into thin strips
2 **spring onions**, cut into thin strips
4 **radishes**, cut into thin strips
25 g (1 oz) **coriander leaves**
50 g (1¾ oz) **wild rocket leaves** (small ones only)
juice of ½ **lemon**

For the beetroot glaze:
200 ml (7 fl oz) **beetroot juice**
4 tbsp **olive oil**

Spicy, Fried Fish Cakes (Tod Man Pla)

Alan Monks

• Finely pound together the chillis, shallot, coriander, lemongrass, lime rind, galangal, salt and pepper in a large mortar and pestle. Add the fish and continue to pound until sticky.

• Transfer to a large bowl, stir in the string beans and kaffir lime leaves, and add the fish sauce. Knead until you can roll the mixture into balls. Flatten each ball into a disk about 1–2.5 cm (½–1 in) thick.

• Heat the vegetable oil in a wok, add the fish cakes and deep fry on each side over a moderate heat until golden. Lift out with a skimmer and drain on some kitchen towels.

• Transfer the fish cakes to a serving plate and garnish with the cucumber, pineapple and tomato. Serve with a separate small dish containing the sweet chilli sauce mixed with the cucumber and peanuts.

Left: Alan Monks with Ziggy, who was rescued from the Cheshire Dogs' Home and enjoys a reputation for eating sausages.

Serves 6

3 **dried chillis**, soaked in water to soften
1 tbsp **shallot**, thinly sliced
1 dessertspoon **powdered coriander**
1 tbsp **lemongrass stalk**, thinly cut
½ tbsp **lime rind**, shredded
½ tbsp **galangal (Thai ginger)**, shredded
1 tsp **salt**
1 tsp **ground pepper**
400 g (14 oz) **cod flesh**, minced
200 g (7 oz) **green string beans**, thinly cut
5 **kaffir lime leaves**, finely shredded
1 tsp **fish sauce**
vegetable oil, for frying
12–18 **cucumber slices**
6 dessertspoons **pineapple**
12–18 **tomato slices**

For the dipping sauce:
6 tbsp **sweet chilli sauce**
12–18 **cucumber slices**
6 tsp **peanuts**, crushed

Butter-bean, Chorizo and Cabbage Soup

Darina Allen

- Heat the olive oil in a sauté pan over a medium heat. Add the onion, cover and sweat until soft but not coloured.
- Toss the chorizo or kabanossi sausage in the pan for 2–3 minutes or until it begins to crisp slightly – the fat should run.
- Chop the tomatoes fairly finely in the tin and add to the pan with the juice. Season with the salt, pepper and sugar, then bring to the boil and cook on a high heat for 5–6 minutes.
- Add the chicken stock and butter-beans, and bring back to the boil. Add the Savoy cabbage and cook for another 2–3 minutes.
- Add the parsley, season to taste and serve with crusty bread.

Serves 6

2 tbsp **extra virgin olive oil**
175 g (6 oz) **onion**, chopped
175 g (6 oz) **chorizo** or
   kabanossi sausage, sliced
1 x 400-g (14-oz) tin of
   tomatoes
salt, freshly ground pepper
   and **sugar**, to taste
1.2 litres (2 pints) **boiling**
   home-made chicken stock
1 x 400-g (14-oz) tin of
   butter-beans, haricot beans
   or **black-eyed beans**
¼ **Savoy cabbage**, thinly sliced
4 tbsp **parsley**, chopped

Opposite: Darina with Sushi and Mimi, her two Jack Russell pups.

Parma Ham with Purple Figs and Minted Yoghurt

James Martin

- Mix the yoghurt and mint, then add the lemon juice and seasoning.
- Arrange each quartered fig on top of some sliced Parma ham in the centre of a plate.
- Drizzle with the minted yoghurt and a little olive oil, season and serve.

Serves 4

For the minted yoghurt:
300 ml (10 fl oz) **Greek yoghurt**
5 g (⅛ oz) **fresh mint,** chopped
juice of 1 **lemon**
salt and **pepper**, to taste

4 **figs**, quartered
225 g (8 oz) **Parma ham**
extra virgin olive oil, to taste

Melon Gazpacho Iced

Stuart Conibear

- Scoop a few 1-cm (½-in) balls from all three melons and set aside, with some mint sprigs, in the freezer.
- Scoop out the rest of the flesh from the melons and blend with the mint. Pass the mixture through a fine strainer, then stir in the Campari and Grenadine. Chill in the freezer.
- Garnish with the reserved melon balls and mint, and serve ice cold.

Serves 8

1 **watermelon**
1 **charentais melon**
1 **galia melon**
100 g (3½ oz) **fresh mint sprigs**
125 ml (4 fl oz) **Campari**
125 ml (4 fl oz) **Grenadine**

Winter Vegetable and Bean Soup with Spicy Sausage

Darina Allen

- After soaking the beans overnight in plenty of cold water, strain and cover with fresh, cold water. Add a bouquet garni and the carrot and onion, and cover and simmer until the beans are soft but not mushy – anywhere from 30–60 minutes.
- Just before the end of cooking, add a little salt. Remove the bouquet garni and vegetables, and discard.
- Blanch the bacon, refresh in cold water and dry well. Put the olive oil in a saucepan, add the bacon and sauté over a medium heat, until crisp and golden.

- Add the onion, carrot and celery, cover and sweat for 5 minutes. Add the parsnip and leek, and cover and sweat for 5 minutes more.
- Add the kabanossi sausage, then chop the tomatoes and add with the haricot beans. Season well and add the chicken stock.
- Cook until the vegetables are tender, about 20 minutes, then taste and correct the seasoning. Sprinkle with the parsley and serve with lots of crusty brown bread.

To cook the beans:
115 g (4 oz) **dried haricot beans**
1 **bouquet garni**
1 **carrot**
1 **onion**

225 g (8 oz) **rindless streaky bacon**, cut into 5-mm (¼-in) lardons
2 tbsp **olive oil**
225 g (8 oz) **onion**, chopped
300 g (10½ oz) **carrot**, cut into 5-mm (¼-in) dice
215 g (7½ oz) **celery**, cut into 5-mm (¼-in) dice
125 g (4½ oz) **parsnip**, cut into 5-mm (¼-in) dice
200 g (7 oz) white part of 1 **leek**, cut into 5-mm (¼-in) slices
1 **kabanossi sausage**, cut into 3-mm (⅛-in) thin slices
1 x 400-g (14-oz) tin of **tomatoes**
salt, **freshly ground pepper** and **sugar**, to taste
1.7 litres (3 pints) **home-made chicken stock**
2 tbsp **parsley**, chopped

Cheese and Bacon Soufflé

Antony Worrall Thompson

Serves 2–4

- Preheat the oven to 200°C/400°F/gas mark 6. Melt 50 g (2 oz) of the butter in a saucepan and butter a soufflé dish with the remainder.
- Add the bacon and onion to the butter in the saucepan and cook until the onion is soft. Add the flour and stir until smooth. Cook for a further 3 minutes, stirring from time to time.
- Slowly add the milk, stirring constantly for 3 minutes until smooth and thick. Season with the salt and cayenne pepper, then add the parmesan cheese.
- Add 4 tablespoons of this sauce to the eggs, then return the egg mixture to the sauce.
- Combine thoroughly, then pour the sauce into the soufflé dish and place in a tray of hot water in the oven. Bake for about 20 minutes, or until set.

75 g (2¾ oz) **unsalted butter**
75 g (2¾ oz) **streaky bacon**, diced
½ **onion**, finely diced
50 g (1¾ oz) **plain flour**
300 ml (½ pint) **hot milk**
salt and **cayenne pepper**, to taste
75 g (2¾ oz) **parmesan cheese**, grated
4 **eggs**, well beaten

Left: Antony Worrall Thompson at home, with his dogs Jessica and Trevor.

Potato, Garlic and Parsley Pie

Paul Heathcote

- Preheat the oven to 200°C/400°F/gas mark 6, then roll out two circles of pastry, one slightly larger than the other. Grease a gratin dish or frying pan and line with the larger pastry circle.
- In a large bowl, mix the potatoes, garlic and parsley, and season with the salt, black pepper and nutmeg. Layer the potatoes in the gratin dish and cover with the remaining pastry circle. Seal the edges, then brush the top with the beaten egg. Cut a cross in the middle to allow the steam to escape, and bake for just under an hour.
- Whisk the egg-yolks and double cream together, remove the pie from the oven and, with a tiny funnel held in the steam hole, slowly pour in the cream mixture. Return to the oven for 10 minutes, then serve flaky triangular wedges hot from the pan.

Serves 6–8

350 g (12 oz) **puff pastry**
450 g (1 lb) **potatoes**, peeled and sliced
3 **garlic cloves**, finely chopped
3 tbsp **flat-leaf parsley**, finely chopped
sea salt, **freshly ground black pepper** and **nutmeg**, to taste
1 **egg**, beaten
2 **egg-yolks**
200 ml (7 fl oz) **double cream**

Tomato Fondue

Darina Allen

- Heat the olive oil in a non-reactive saucepan. Add the onion and garlic, toss until coated, then cover and sweat on a gentle heat until soft but not coloured. It is essential that the onion is completely soft before you add the tomatoes.
- Slice the tomatoes and add to the onion with the juice. Season well (the tinned tomatoes will need lots of sugar to counteract their acidity), then add a generous sprinkling of herbs.
- Cook uncovered for 10–20 minutes more, or until the tomatoes soften. Fresh tomatoes require a shorter cooking time than tinned tomatoes to preserve their lively, fresh flavour.

Serves 6

1 tbsp **extra virgin olive oil**
115 g (4 oz) **onion**, sliced
1 **garlic clove**, crushed
900 g (2 lb) very ripe **tomatoes** or 2 x 400-g (14-oz) tin of **tomatoes**, peeled
salt, **freshly ground pepper** and **sugar**, to taste
1 tbsp **mint**, **thyme**, **parsley**, **lemon balm**, **marjoram** or **torn basil**, freshly chopped

Twice-Baked Lancashire Soufflés

Nigel Haworth

- First, brush the ramekins from the inside out with a little butter, then coat with the almonds. Set aside.
- To prepare the soufflés, melt the butter in a heavy-bottomed pan, then add the flour. Cook without colouring for 1–2 minutes. Add the milk a little at a time and stir until smooth. Cook for a further 2 minutes over a medium-high heat.
- Add the Lancashire cheese and blend in well. Remove the pan from the stove, allow the contents to cool slightly, then add the egg-yolks. Transfer to a stainless-steel bowl.
- In a separate bowl, whisk the egg-white with a pinch of salt until it forms soft peaks. Gradually fold into the Lancashire-cheese mixture. Spoon into the ramekins, then place in the oven in a tray of hot water and cook for 12–15 minutes at 180°C/350°F/gas mark 4.
- Remove the ramekins from the oven and allow them to cool. Then remove the soufflés and place on a silicon paper-lined tray to cool before refrigerating. Set the ramekins aside.
- Put the cherry tomatoes in a baking dish and sprinkle over the icing sugar and salt. Half cover with the olive oil and bake in the oven for 5 minutes at 160°C/325°F/gas mark 3.
- Remove the soufflés from the refrigerator. Place a dessertspoon of whipping cream in each ramekin and top with a soufflé. Place the ramekins on a baking tray and bake for 5 minutes at 180–200°C/350–400°F/gas mark 4–6. To serve, divide the cherry tomatoes among 8 plates. Place a baked soufflé in the middle of each plate and garnish with the salad leaves.

Serves 8

To line the ramekin dishes:
50 g (1¾ oz) **unsalted butter**, softened
100 g (3½ oz) **ground almonds**

40 g (1½ oz) **unsalted butter**
50 g (1¾ oz) **plain flour**
250 ml (9 fl oz) **boiling milk**
160 g (5¾ oz) **Lancashire cheese**
2 **egg-yolks**
125 g (4½ oz) **egg-white**
8 dessertspoons **whipping cream**
100 g (3½ oz) **salad leaves dressed with olive oil**, to taste

For the sweet-and-sour cherry tomatoes:
1 punnet **cherry tomatoes**
40 g (1½ oz) **icing sugar**
5 g (⅛ oz) **salt**
100 ml (3½ fl oz) **olive oil**

Chargrilled Red Mullet with Spicy, Sunny Savoy Cabbage

Ainsley Harriott

- Place the red mullet fillets in a dish and drizzle with the lime juice and zest, and 2 tablespoons of the olive oil. Leave to marinate.
- Meanwhile, heat the remaining tablespoon of olive oil and the butter in a large frying pan or wok for the cabbage. Heat the chargrill pan for the mullet.
- Add the ginger and chilli pepper to the frying pan, and stir-fry for 30 seconds, followed by the bacon for a further 30 seconds.
- Add the carrot and stir-fry for 1 minute. Add the cabbage, mix well and cook for 2–3 minutes more. Pour over the soy sauce and honey, and adjust the seasoning.
- While the cabbage is cooking, place the red mullet fillets skin-side down into the chargrill pan and cook for 2–3 minutes, turning once during this time.
- Lightly dust the rims of your plates with a pinch of cayenne, then sprinkle over the chives.
- Place a pile of the spicy cabbage in the centre of each plate, then lay the red mullet fillets on top. Drizzle with a little olive oil, add a touch of black pepper and serve with a glass of crisp white wine.

Serves 2–4

4 x 75–100g (2¾–3½ oz) **red mullet fillet**
zest and juice of 1 **lime**
3 tbsp **olive oil**
25 g (1 oz) **unsalted butter**
2.5-cm (1-in) piece of **root ginger**
1 **small red chilli pepper**, seeded and sliced into rounds
2 **smoked bacon rashers**, rinded and cut into fine strips
100 g (3½ oz) **carrot**, peeled and cut into fine matchsticks
225g (8 oz) **Savoy** or **white cabbage**, finely sliced
2 tbsp **soy sauce**
1 tbsp **clear honey**
salt and **freshly ground black pepper**, to taste
cayenne, for plate dusting
1 tbsp **chives**, freshly chopped

Opposite: Ainsley Harriott with Oscar.

Roasted Salmon Fillets with a Pecorino and Pesto Topping

Delia Smith

- Preheat the oven to 230°C/450°F/gas mark 8. You will need a baking tray measuring 25 x 35 cm (10 x 14 in), covered in foil and lightly oiled.
- Begin by trimming the fillets if needed, and run your hand over the surface of the fish to check that there aren't any stray bones lurking. Now place the fillets on the prepared baking tray and give each one a good squeeze of lemon juice and a seasoning of salt and black pepper.
- Next, give the pesto a good stir, mix it with one-third of the breadcrumbs to form a paste and spread this over both fish fillets. Then mix half of the pecorino cheese with the remaining bread-crumbs and scatter this over the pesto. Finish off with the remaining pecorino cheese.
- Now place the baking tray on the middle shelf of the oven and cook for 10 minutes, by which time the top should be golden brown and crispy, and the salmon just cooked and moist. Serve with steamed new potatoes.

Serves 2

2 x 150–175-g (5½–6-oz) **salmon fillet**, about 2 cm (¾ in) thick, skinned
juice of ½ lemon
salt and **freshly ground black pepper**
2 level tbsp **fresh pesto sauce**
2 level tbsp **fresh bread-crumbs**
1 rounded tbsp **pecorino cheese**, finely grated

Black Pepper Prawns (Jheenga Kali Mirch)

K. K. Anand

- Peel the prawns, leaving the tails on and reserving the shells for the prawn stock. Then split the prawns down the centre so they open like butterflies. De-vein and thoroughly refresh in cold water.
- Make a prawn stock by placing the shells in a saucepan with 500 ml (18 fl oz) of water and simmering for about 15 minutes. Be sure to drain the stock and discard the shells before using.
- Meanwhile, put the cooking oil into a heavy-bottomed pan and warm over a medium heat. Add the onions, garlic and ginger, and sauté until light brown.
- Add the turmeric and paprika, and stir for a minute. Then add the tomatoes and cook for a further 3–4 minutes.
- Slide the prawns in slowly and continue stirring. Add the salt, black pepper and prawn stock, and cook for 5–6 minutes.
- When the prawns' tails turn red, signifying that they are fully cooked, add the single cream and let simmer for another 2 minutes. Stir in the coriander and serve hot.

Serves 2

8 **king prawns**, size 6–8 and headless
4 tbsp **cooking oil**
3 **medium-sized onions**, chopped
1 tbsp **garlic**, chopped
1 tbsp **ginger**, chopped
½ tsp **turmeric**
1 tsp **paprika**
2 **medium-sized tomatoes**, chopped
salt, to taste
1 tbsp **crushed black pepper**
1 tbsp **single cream**
1 tbsp **coriander**, chopped

Cornish Dived Scallops with Braised Oxtail

Nathan Outlaw

- Roast the oxtail in the oven for 1 hour at 200°C/400°F/gas mark 6.
- Meanwhile, warm the oil in a pan big enough to hold the oxtail and all of the other ingredients. Add the onion, carrots and garlic, and cook for 2–3 minutes, or until lightly coloured. Add the red wine, chicken stock and thyme, bring to a simmer and skim off any impurities.
- When the oxtail is cooked, add to the pan and simmer for 2 hours, or until the meat comes away from the bone easily. Pick off the meat, strain the vegetables and reduce the liquid until about 200 ml (7 fl oz) remains. Skim off any impurities as they appear.
- To prepare the potato and apple purée, simmer the potatoes for 20 minutes, or until cooked through. Strain and set aside, covering to keep warm. Put the apple into a pan with the butter and double cream, and cook for about 5 minutes, until softened. Mash the potato and apple together, and season.
- In a separate bowl, blend the pickled walnuts, pickled walnut juice, olive oil, sage, apple and a little salt and pepper, and set aside.
- Next, prepare the scallops. Rinse in cold water, gently pat dry and season well.
- Put 1 tablespoon of oil in a non-stick pan. When very hot, add the scallops and cook on one side for 3 minutes, then on the other for a further 3 minutes. Allow to rest for 2 minutes.
- Just before serving, reheat the oxtail, in its juice, with the walnut and sage dressing. Heat the purée and place on a plate with the scallops, then spoon over the oxtail and dressing.

Serves 4

1 kg (2 lb 4 oz) **oxtail on the bone** (centre cut)
100 ml (3½ fl oz) **oil**
1 **onion**, chopped
2 **carrots**, chopped
1 **garlic clove**
1 litre (1¾ pints) **red wine**
1 litre (1¾ pints) **cold chicken stock**
50 g (1¾ oz) **thyme**
12 **scallops**
salt and **pepper**, to taste

For the potato and apple purée:
500 g (1 lb 2 oz) **potatoes**
1 **Bramley apple**, chopped
50 g (1¾ oz) **unsalted butter**
50 ml (2 fl oz) **double cream**

For the pickled walnut and sage dressing:
50 g (1¾ oz) **pickled walnuts**, finely chopped
50 ml (2 fl oz) **pickled walnut juice**
100 ml (3½ fl oz) **olive oil**
25 g (1 oz) **sage**, chopped
50 g (1¾ oz) **Granny Smith apple**, chopped

Steamed Wild Sea Bass with Pastis and Saffron Sauce

Morgan Meunier

- Blanch the asparagus for 2 minutes in hot, salted water.
- Then, in an oven preheated to 180°C/350°F/gas mark 6, cook the razor clams for 2 minutes, or until open. Add the tomato, shallot and olive oil, and cook for another minute.
- Blanch the baby fennel in hot, salted water, then split and grill until very dark in colour.
- To prepare the sauce, sweat the fennel, star anise, shallots, carrots and celery in a pan with the butter for about 5 minutes, then add the fish stock and saffron. Reduce to a glaze, then pour in the double cream. Add the juice from the oranges and lemon, and the Pastis, and bring back to the boil just before serving.
- Steam the wild sea bass for 5 minutes. To serve, put the razor clams back in their shells and place on a plate with the sea bass. Pour over the sauce.

Serves 8

1 bunch of **asparagus**
250 g (9 oz) **razor clams**
1 **tomato**, diced
1 **shallot**, diced
2 tbsp **olive oil**
4 **baby fennel**
1 x 2 kg (4 lb 8 oz) **wild sea bass**, skinned, filleted and pin boned

For the sauce:
1 **fennel**
3 **star anise**
5 **shallots**
5 **carrots**
2 **celery sticks**
25 g (1 oz) **butter**
2 litres (3½ pints) **cold fish stock**
½ tsp **saffron**
100 ml (3½ fl oz) **double cream**
juice of 2 **oranges**
juice of 1 **lemon**
3 tbsp **Pastis** or **Pernod**

Grilled Haddock with Mustard, Lentil and Celeriac Sauce

Shaun Hill

• Boil the celeriac for 30 minutes, or until soft, then mash. Season with a little salt and pepper, and add the double cream.

• Next, boil the brown lentils until very soft. This will take about 10 minutes if they have been presoaked, and 30 minutes if not. Drain.

• Warm the oil in a pan over a moderate heat, then add the shallot and bacon. Fry until soft, about 5 minutes. Add the brown lentils, fry for a further 5 minutes and season to taste.

• In a separate pan, bring the chicken stock, crème fraîche and wholegrain mustard to the boil, then thicken with the butter. Season with the lemon juice, then add the braised lentils.

• Grill the haddock fillets until done, turning once during cooking. To serve, place each fillet on a mound of celeriac and pour the mustard and lentil sauce around it.

Serves 4

400 g (14 oz) **celeriac,** peeled and cubed
salt and **pepper**, to taste
25 ml (1 oz) **double cream**
20 g (¾ oz) **brown lentils**
1 tbsp **oil**
1 **shallot**, chopped
1 **streaky bacon rasher**, finely diced
100 ml (3½ fl oz) **cold chicken stock**
250 ml (9 fl oz) **crème fraîche**
1 tbsp **wholegrain mustard**
30 g (1¼ oz) **unsalted butter**
1 tbsp **lemon juice**
4 x 200 g (7 oz) **haddock fillet**

Left: Shaun Hill with Franco.

Fried Noodles with Teriyaki Salmon

Anton Edelmann

- Place the salmon in a dish and pour the teriyaki marinade over it. Marinate for 30 minutes, turning the salmon a couple of times.
- Next, cook the noodles in slightly salted water for the length of time indicated on the packet. Strain, refresh in cold water and drain.
- Drain the salmon, reserving the marinade, and grill the fillets for approximately 2 minutes on either side. They should remain pink in the middle.

- Heat a wok or non-stick pan and add the oil. Add the spring onions and garlic, and sweat for 30 seconds. Then add the turnip and tomato purée, and sweat for a further 30 seconds.
- Add the noodles, paprika and reserved marinade with the lime juice. Cook for a further minute, stirring continuously.
- Add the peanuts and alfalfa, then transfer to 4 bowls. Top with the salmon fillets and serve.

Serves 4

350 g (12 oz) **salmon fillet**, skin and bones removed and cut into 70-g (2½-oz) pieces at a slant

100 ml (3½ fl oz) **teriyaki marinade**

225 g (8 oz) **rice** or **egg noodles**

4 tsp **oil**

2 **spring onions**, washed and sliced

2 **garlic cloves**, peeled and crushed

150 g (5½ oz) **turnip**, peeled and cubed

½ tsp **tomato purée**

½ tsp **paprika**

juice of 1 **lime**

25 g (1 oz) **peanuts**, finely chopped

50 g (1¾ oz) **alfalfa** or **bean sprouts**

salt and **freshly ground pepper**, to taste

Confit of Wild Salmon with Watercress Risotto

Jake Watkins

- First, bring a large pan of salted water to the boil. Pick the watercress leaves and plunge into the salted water, then immediately into iced water.
- Drain the leaves and dry with a clean tea towel. Then liquidise in a blender with 100 ml (3½ fl oz) of the vegetable stock until smooth. Set aside.
- Prepare the risotto by gently frying the shallots and garlic in the butter until well cooked but not coloured. Add the arborio rice and stir well, ensuring that the rice is completely coated in butter. Season with the salt and pepper.
- Add the remaining 400 ml (14 fl oz) of the vegetable stock a ladle at a time and stir. Repeat until the rice is just cooked, then spread on a tray to cool.
- To prepare the velouté, fry the shallots, leek and garlic in the butter until well cooked but not coloured. Add the white wine and boil until one-third remains.
- Add the fish stock and boil until half remains. Add the double cream and horseradish, and simmer for 5 minutes. Pour through a fine sieve.
- To prepare the salmon, warm the olive oil in a pan until it reaches about 90°C/195°F/gas mark ¼. Add the fish portions and poach for 12 minutes, so they remain slightly pink.
- Warm the risotto, then add the double cream and parmesan cheese. Stir in the watercress purée and cover to keep warm.
- Warm the velouté and whisk vigorously to achieve a cappuccino-like effect. Spread the watercress risotto on a large plate, then season the salmon portions with a little salt and lemon juice. Place the fish on top of the risotto, spoon over the velouté and serve.

Serves 4

For the watercress purée:
4 bunches of **watercress**
500 ml (18 fl oz) **cold vegetable stock**

For the risotto:
4 **shallots**, chopped
½ **garlic clove**
50 g (1¾ oz) **unsalted butter**
100 g (3½ oz) **arborio rice**
salt and **pepper**, to taste
50 ml (2 fl oz) **double cream**
50 g (1¾ oz) **parmesan cheese**, freshly grated

For the velouté:
4 **shallots**, finely sliced
¼ **leek**, finely sliced
½ **garlic clove**, finely sliced
50 g (1¾ oz) **unsalted butter**
150 ml (5 fl oz) **white wine**
250 ml (9 fl oz) **cold fish stock**
250 ml (9 oz) **double cream**
1 tbsp **horseradish**, grated

500 ml (18 fl oz) **olive oil**
4 x 100-g (3½-oz) **wild salmon portion**
lemon juice, to taste

Stir-Fried Salt and Pepper Squid

Rick Stein

- Clean the squid, then cut along one side of each pouch and open out flat. Score the inner side into a diamond pattern with the tip of a small, sharp knife, then cut into 5-cm (2-in) squares. Separate the tentacles if large, and set to one side.
- For the salad, cut the cucumber lengthways into short, thin strips. Toss in a bowl with the bean sprouts and watercress. In a separate bowl, whisk together the soy sauce, sesame oil, caster sugar and a little salt.
- Heat a heavy-bottomed frying pan over a high heat, add the black peppercorns and Sichuan peppercorns, and dry roast for a few seconds, shaking the pan now and then until they darken slightly and start to smell aromatic. Tip into a mortar, coarsely crush with the pestle and stir in the Maldon salt.
- Heat a wok over a high heat until it smokes. Add half of the sunflower oil and half of the squid, and stir-fry for 2 minutes. Tip on to a plate and repeat with the rest of the oil and squid.
- Return the first batch of squid to the wok and add 1 teaspoon of

the salt and pepper mixture. Toss for 10 seconds, then add the red finger chilli and spring onions. Toss again, then divide among 4 plates, making slightly off-centre piles. Dress the salad, pile alongside the squid and serve.

Serves 4

750 g (1 lb 10 oz) **squid**, unprepared
½ tsp **black peppercorns**
½ tsp **Sichuan peppercorns**
1 tsp **Maldon salt**
2 tbsp **sunflower oil**
1 **medium-hot red finger chilli**, thinly sliced (seeds removed if you prefer)
3 **spring onions**, trimmed and sliced

For the salad:
1 **cucumber**, peeled, halved and the seeds removed
50 g (1¾ oz) **fresh bean sprouts**
25 g (1 oz) **watercress sprigs**, large stalks removed
1 tsp **dark soy sauce**
2 tsp **roasted sesame oil**
¼ tsp **caster sugar**
salt, to taste

Left: Rick Stein with his cookery programme co-star, Chalky.

Penne with Pancetta and Flat-Leaf Parsley

James Martin

- Place the Pancetta in a pan with the olive oil and fry until nice and crisp.
- Meanwhile, put the penne pasta in a large pan of boiling, salted water, return to the boil, then simmer for 10–12 minutes, or until the pasta is soft.
- While the pasta is cooking, mix the egg-yolks and double cream in a bowl with the parmesan cheese. Season well and add the flat-leaf parsley.
- Drain the pasta and quickly add to the ingredients in the bowl, with a little olive oil and seasoning. Stir well, then serve in a bowl with some parmesan cheese shavings and black pepper on top.

Serves 4–6

175 g (6 oz) **Pancetta**, diced
2 tbsp **virgin olive oil**
250 g (9 oz) **penne pasta**
3 **free-range egg-yolks**
100 ml (3½ fl oz) **double cream**
175 g (6 oz) **parmesan cheese**, freshly grated
Maldon salt and **freshly ground black pepper**, to taste
6 tbsp **flat-leaf parsley**, chopped

Opposite: James Martin with Fudge.

Spicy Sausage with Pasta and Vegetables

Anton Edelmann

- Cook the fusilli pasta in boiling, slightly salted water until al dente, then refresh and drain well.
- Heat the onion in a little olive oil over a medium heat for 30 seconds, then add the garlic and chilli pepper. Cook until soft and translucent, then add the chorizo and sweat for a further 2–3 minutes.
- Add the white wine and bring to the boil. Remove the chorizo and set aside, covering to keep warm.
- Reduce the white wine by half and add the double cream and sage stalks. Reduce by half again, then remove the sage stalks.
- Add the Savoy cabbage, broccoli and carrot, then cover and simmer gently until tender. Add the chorizo and fusilli pasta, and season with a little salt and pepper.
- Heat the remaining olive oil in a separate pan, add the sage leaves and fry until nice and crisp.
- To serve, spoon the pasta mixture into 4 bowls, garnish with the sage leaves and parmesan cheese shavings, and drizzle a little sage oil all over.

Serves 4

200 g (7 oz) **fusilli pasta**
1 **onion**, peeled and finely chopped
40 ml (1½ fl oz) **olive oil**
2 **garlic cloves**, peeled and crushed
1 **chilli pepper**, finely chopped
200 g (7 oz) **chorizo**, skin removed and cut into slices
200 ml (7 fl oz) **white wine**
100 ml (3½ fl oz) **double cream**
3 **sage stalks** (leaves reserved)
¼ **Savoy cabbage,** stalk removed and blanched
100 g (3½ fl oz) **broccoli**, blanched
100 g (3½ fl oz) **carrot,** peeled and sliced
salt and **freshly ground pepper**, to taste
parmesan cheese shavings, to taste
sage oil, to taste

Linguine with Loch Linnhe Langoustines

Allan and Eileen Donald

• Cook the linguine in a pan of boiling, salted water for about 8 minutes, or until al dente, then refresh and drain well.

• Heat 1 tablespoon of the olive oil in a pan until it starts to smoke. Add the langoustines and sauté for 1 minute on each side. Remove from the pan and set aside.

• In another pan, heat the remaining tablespoon of the oil until it smokes. Add the langoustine shells, garlic and shallots, and sauté for 3–4 minutes.

• Add the tomato purée and chicken stock. Bring to the boil and simmer until reduced by half. Add the double cream and simmer for 5 minutes. Pour the sauce through a fine sieve, then season to taste.

• Return the sauce to the pan and stir in the linguine, garden peas, tarragon leaves and langoustines. Gently heat to warm through, season and serve immediately.

Serves 4

200 g (7 oz) **dried linguine**
2 tbsp **olive oil**
20 **langoustines,** shelled and de-veined (shells reserved)
1 **garlic clove**, crushed
2 **shallots**, finely chopped
25 g (1 oz) **tomato purée**
600 ml (1 pint) **cold chicken stock**
600 ml (1 pint) **double cream**
salt and **freshly ground black pepper**, to taste
50 g (1¾ oz) **garden peas,** blanched
15 g (½ oz) **tarragon leaves**

Green Pea and Smoked Salmon Risotto

James Martin

- Sweat the shallot and garlic in a pan with the butter until soft but not coloured. Add the arborio rice and cook for a further 30 seconds over a low heat to seal.
- Add the white wine and cook for a few seconds more. Then add the fish stock and chicken stock a little at a time. Simmer for 12 minutes, stirring continuously.
- When the risotto is finished cooking, stir in the mascarpone cheese, smoked salmon, peas, parmesan cheese and flat-leaf parsley. Season well.
- Spoon the risotto on to the centre of a plate and top with a little parmesan cheese. Drizzle with a little olive oil and serve immediately.

Serves 4–6

1 **shallot**, peeled and chopped
1 **garlic clove**, peeled and chopped
25 g (1 oz) **unsalted butter**
250 g (1¾ oz) **arborio rice**
50 ml (2 fl oz) **white wine**
500 ml (18 fl oz) **warm fish stock**
500 ml (18 fl oz) **warm chicken stock**
100 g (3½ oz) **mascarpone cheese**
8 oz (225 g) **smoked salmon**, sliced
150 g (5½ oz) **frozen peas**
100 g (3½ oz) **parmesan cheese**, freshly grated
10 g (¼ oz) **flat-leaf parsley**, chopped
salt and **pepper**, to taste
olive oil, to taste

Warm Salad of Honey and Mustard Glazed Chicken

Chris and James Tanner

- Stir together the honey and grain mustard in a bowl, add the chicken slices and mix until well coated.
- Put the chicken slices in a hot chargrill pan, cook for 3–4 minutes on each side, then set aside.
- Drizzle a little olive over the rocket salad, season with a little salt and pepper, and place in the centre of a serving dish.
- Stack the chicken on top of the salad leaves, crumble goat's cheese over the top and sprinkle with the pine nuts. Drizzle a little honey around the salad and serve.

Serves 1–2

2 tbsp **clear honey**
1 dessertspoon **grain mustard**
1 **chicken breast**, skinned and sliced
olive oil, to taste
1 bunch of **rocket salad**, washed
salt and **pepper**, to taste
150 g (5 fl oz) **goat's cheese**
100 g (3 ½ fl oz) **pine nuts**, toasted

Breast of Duckling with Fresh Berries and Apple Mash

Serves 4

For the apple mash:
500 g (1 lb 2 oz) **Bramley apples**, peeled, cored and diced
50 g (1¾ oz) **caster sugar**
200 ml (7 fl oz) **double cream**
100 g (3½ oz) **unsalted butter**
1 kg (2 lb 4 oz) **dry mashed potatoes**
salt and **pepper**, to taste

For the duck jus:
1 kg (2 lb 4 oz) **duck bones**
200 g (7 oz) **mirepoix**, including 50 g (1¾ oz) each of **carrot**, **celery**, **onion** and **leek**, all diced
20 g (¾ oz) **fresh thyme**
2 **fresh bay leaves**
10 g (¼ oz) **fresh garlic**
100 ml (3½ fl oz) **Madeira**
100 ml (3½ fl oz) **port**
150 ml (5 fl oz) **red wine**
5 litres (8¾ pints) **chicken stock**
1 **cinnamon stick**
2 **juniper berries** (optional)

4 **Gressingham duckling breasts**
20 g (¾ oz) **fresh pear**, peeled and diced
20 g (¾ oz) **mango**, peeled and diced
20 g (¾ oz) **peach**, peeled and diced
40 g (1½ oz) **fresh strawberries**, quartered
20 g (¾ oz) **fresh blueberries**
20 g (¾ oz) **red currants**
25 g (1 oz) **raspberries**
25 g (1 oz) **blackberries**
fresh basil leaves, for garnishing
fresh mint leaves, for garnishing

Stuart Conibear

• First, prepare the apple mash. Place the apples, caster sugar and a little water in a heavy-bottomed pan and bring to the boil. Remove the pan from the heat and allow the ingredients to cook out until the apple has completely softened.

• Transfer to a blender and purée until smooth.

• In a separate pan, bring the double cream and butter to the boil and add the dry mashed potatoes, purée and a little seasoning. Set aside.

• To prepare the duck jus, place the duck bones and mirepoix in a roasting tray and cook in the oven for 20–30 minutes at 160°C/325°F/gas mark 3.

• Add the thyme, bay leaves and garlic, and season. Then deglaze the roasting tray with the Madeira, port and red wine, and reduce until no liquid remains.

• Add the chicken stock and bring back to the boil. Reduce by two-thirds, skimming off any impurities as they appear.

• Remove the roasting tray from the heat, add the cinnamon stick and juniper berries, if available, and cover with cling film for 20 minutes to allow the aromas to infuse the sauce.

• Pass through a fine sieve, discard the trimmings and return the sauce to the stove. Bring back to the boil, skimming off any impurities as they appear and adjusting the seasoning. Pass through a double layer of muslin and set aside.

• Next, brown the duckling breasts in a hot,

non-stick frying pan skin-side down for 1 minute, then underneath for a further 4 minutes. Place in the oven and cook to rare, about 5–8 minutes. Remove from the oven and set aside to rest.

• Meanwhile, seal the pear, mango, peach and strawberries in a hot frying pan with a little butter for 30 seconds, or until they just start to break down. Remove the pan from the heat and add the blueberries, red currants, raspberries and blackberries.

• Reheat the apple mash, add seasoning and place in a piping bag. Reheat the duck jus.

• Pipe the mash on to the centre of 4 plates. Slice the duckling breasts into 3 portions each and place on top of the mash, skin-side down. Pour over the fruit, then drizzle the sauce around. Finish by sprinkling over the basil and mint leaves.

Roasted Corn-Fed Chicken with New Season Garlic

Ben McKellar

- First, preheat the oven to 200°C/400°F/gas mark 6. Season the chicken and place in a roasting dish with the garlic, thyme and olive oil. Roast for about 1–1½ hours, or until the juices run clear. Don't forget to baste the chicken.
- Remove the chicken from the roasting dish and allow to rest. Set aside half of the garlic and crush the rest with a fork. Deglaze the roasting dish with the white wine and reduce the sauce by half. Then add the chicken stock and reduce by half again.
- Strain the sauce and add the rest of the garlic. Season well and pour over the carved chicken. Mashed potatoes and spinach complement this dish nicely.

Serves 4

salt and **pepper**, to taste
1 x 2.25 kg (5 lb) **corn-fed chicken**
4 heads of **new season garlic**, separated
1 bunch of **thyme**, chopped
2 tbsp **olive oil**
1 glass **white wine**
600 ml (1 pint) **chicken stock**

Peppered Chicken Salad

Ainsley Harriott

- Preheat the oven to 200°C/400°F/gas mark 6, then heat a griddle pan and oil it with a little lemon oil. Cut the ciabatta roll in half and drizzle the insides with olive oil. Sprinkle with rock salt and set aside.
- Place the chicken breasts in a large bag and bash with a rolling pin until flattened. Remove from the bag and brush each piece with a little lemon oil.
- Crush the mixed, coloured peppercorns in a pestle and mortar, and sprinkle them over the chicken. Place the breasts in the griddle pan and cook for 4–5 minutes, turning once during cooking.
- Heat the lemon oil in a separate, small pan. Crush in the garlic, then add the ginger with the lime zest and fry for about a minute. Add the white wine to the pan and boil rapidly until reduced by half.
- Meanwhile, mix the avocado, red onion and cherry tomatoes in a bowl with the salad leaves. Remove the chicken breasts from the pan and slice diagonally into strips. Pop the slices of ciabatta roll upside down on to the hot griddle and char.

- Cut the zested lime in half and squeeze the juice into the pan with the garlic and ginger reduction mixture. Tear in the coriander leaves and simmer for 1 minute.
- Arrange the salad leaves on a serving place. Pile the chicken in the middle, drizzle over the remaining reduction mixture and serve with the warm, charred ciabatta roll.

Serves 2

2 tbsp **lemon oil**
1 **ciabatta roll**
olive oil, to taste
rock salt, to taste
2 **small chicken breasts**, skinned
2 tsp **mixed, coloured whole peppercorns**
1 **garlic clove**
2.5-cm (1-in) piece of **fresh root ginger**, unpeeled
zest of 1 **lime** (lime reserved)
125 ml (4 fl oz) **white wine**
1 **small avocado**, peeled, stoned and sliced
½ **small red onion**, sliced
5 **cherry tomatoes**, halved
70-g (2½-oz) small bag of **crispy green salad leaves**
fresh coriander, to taste

Poussin with Asparagus

Raymond Patterson

- Remove the bones from the poussin legs and breasts, and set the meat aside.
- Place the bones in a large pan and cover with water. Add the thyme, garlic, shallots and celery, and bring to the boil. Simmer for 10–15 minutes to reduce the stock by half, skimming off any impurities as they appear.
- While the stock is simmering, slow roast the meat from the poussin legs in the oven for 8 minutes at 200°C/400°F/gas mark 6.
- Pan fry the breasts, with the tarragon and seasoning, in a little olive oil and butter for 4–5 minutes.
- To serve, pass the stock through a fine chinois and pour into a large bowl. Add the poussin meat, asparagus, potatoes and eggs, and sprinkle with a little thyme.

Serves 2

2 **poussin**
3 **thyme sprigs** (a little reserved for garnishing)
4 **garlic cloves**, roughly chopped
4 **shallots**, roughly chopped
2 **celery stalks**, roughly chopped
3 **tarragon sprigs**, roughly chopped
salt and **pepper**, to taste
olive oil and **butter**, for frying
6 **asparagus stalks**, boiled for 3 minutes
8 **Jersey Royal potatoes**, boiled until cooked through
2 **eggs**, poached

Chicken Tikka Masala

James Martin

- Place the chicken in a large bowl and mix with the ginger, garlic, chilli powder, sea salt, black pepper, coriander, lime juice and 1 tablespoon of the vegetable oil. Set aside to allow the flavours to develop.
- Heat a shallow, heavy-bottomed pan and, when hot, add the chicken. Cook for 8–10 minutes, or until browned on all sides.
- Meanwhile, heat the remaining vegetable oil in a large pan over a medium heat and cook the onion and red chilli for 5–6 minutes, until golden brown. Add the turmeric and cook for 1 minute. Stir in the double cream and cook gently for a few minutes more.
- Add the chicken to the creamy sauce. Simmer for 5 minutes, until cooked through. Adjust the seasoning and add the lemon juice to taste. Garnish with the coriander and serve immediately with some rice or naan bread.

Serves 4–6

4 **chicken breasts**, skinned, boned and cubed
2.5-cm (1-in) piece of **root ginger**, finely chopped
2 **garlic cloves**, finely chopped
1 tsp **chilli powder**
sea salt and **freshly ground black pepper**, to taste
2 tbsp **fresh coriander**
juice of 1 **lime**
2 tbsp **vegetable oil**
1 **onion**, finely chopped
1 **red chilli**, seeded and finely chopped
1 tsp **ground turmeric**
300 ml (10 fl oz) **double cream**
juice of ½ **lemon**
fresh coriander, to garnish
naan bread or **rice**, to serve

Salad of Spring Lamb Niçoise-Style with Egg Dressing

Chris and James Tanner

- Cut the garlic in half and rub over the lamb fillets. Then coat the meat with the rosemary, salt, pepper and olive oil, and cook in a chargrill pan for 2–3 minutes on each side. Set aside.
- To make the egg dressing, place the eggs in a bowl, add the lemon juice and whisk in a little olive oil. Season with the salt and pepper, and top with the parsley
- To prepare the salad, gently warm the aubergine, courgette, red pepper, new potatoes, plum tomatoes and black olives in a saucepan. Transfer to a large bowl and mix with the anchovies, rocket salad, Balsamic vinegar, olive oil and croutons.
- Slice the lamb fillets and arrange on top of the salad. Spoon over the egg dressing just before serving.

Serves 2

2 **garlic cloves**
4 **lamb fillets**
2 **rosemary sprigs**, chopped
salt and **pepper**, to taste
4 tbsp **olive oil**

For the egg dressing:
2 **eggs**, boiled for 3 minutes, peeled and mashed
juice of ½ lemon
parsley sprigs, chopped, to taste

For the salad:
6 **aubergine pieces**, chargrilled
8 **courgette slices**, chargrilled
1 **red pepper slice**, chargrilled
3 **new potatoes**, cooked and sliced
2 **plum tomatoes**, diced and de-seeded
1 handful of **pitted black olives**
8 **marinated anchovy fillets**
2 handfuls of **rocket salad**
1 tbsp **Balsamic vinegar**
2 tbsp **olive oil**
croutons, to garnish

Roasted Lamb Loin with Chorizo

Matt Watts

- To prepare the red wine reduction, sweat the onion, celery and garlic in half of the olive oil for 10 minutes over a low heat, or until thoroughly softened.

- Add the tomatoes, Balsamic vinegar and port, and reduce until a syrup or glaze remains. Add the red wine and slowly reduce by half, skimming off any impurities as they appear.

- Strain the sauce through a fine sieve, then continue simmering until reduced to about 100 ml (3½ fl oz).

- To prepare the lamb loins, preheat the oven to about 190°C–200°C/375°F–400°F/gas mark 5–6. Heat the remaining olive oil in a pan and fry the meat until sealed and coloured all over.

- Transfer to the oven and cook for 6–8 minutes. Remove from the oven, cover to keep warm and set aside.

- Meanwhile, sauté the black pudding, chorizo, new potatoes and spring cabbage in the butter, seasoning to taste. Cook for 2–3 minutes, or until the cabbage is just cooked, bright and green.

- Slice the lamb and reheat the red wine reduction.

- To assemble the dish, divide the cabbage mixture among 4 warmed plates, top with one of the sliced lamb loins and spoon over some red wine reduction. Add a little pesto and aioli, if you like, and decorate with the rosemary.

Serves 4

For the red wine reduction:
1 **onion**, peeled and chopped
1 **celery stalk**, peeled and chopped
5 **garlic cloves**, peeled and chopped
85 ml (3 fl oz) **olive oil**
2 **tomatoes**, chopped
3 tbsp **Balsamic vinegar**
2 tbsp **port**
1 bottle of **red wine**

4 x 225 g (8 oz) **lamb loin**, trimmed
100 g (3½ oz) **black pudding**, cut into cubes
100 g (3½ oz) **chorizo**, cut into cubes
10–14 **new potatoes**, lightly boiled and cut into slices
½–1 **spring cabbage**, finely shredded
55 g (2 oz) **unsalted butter**
salt and **pepper**, to taste
2 tbsp **pesto** or **herb oil** (optional)
1 tbsp **aioli** (optional)
4 **rosemary sprigs**

Pan-Grilled Lamb Cutlets (Masala Champey)

K. K. Anand

Serves 2

- Place the lamb cutlets in a large bag and pound with a rolling pin until flattened.
- In a large bowl, mix half of the ginger garlic paste, half of the red chilli powder, the Greek yoghurt and salt. Stir in the lamb cutlets, then set aside for at least 30 minutes to let the flavours develop.
- Heat 2 tablespoons of the vegetable oil in a pan and fry the lamb cutlets for 10 minutes over a low heat. Alternatively, grill them in the oven for 10 minutes at 180°C/350°F/gas mark 4.
- In a separate pan, heat the remaining 4 tablespoons of the vegetable oil and add the onions. Cook until light brown, then add the remaining ginger garlic paste, the remaining chilli powder, a little salt and the tomato purée.
- Cook for 5 minutes, then stir in the cutlets. Simmer for a further 5 minutes and add the garam masala and ginger. Remove from the heat and serve hot.

8 **lamb cutlets**
1 tbsp **ginger garlic paste**
2 tsp **red chilli powder**
2 tbsp **Greek yoghurt**
salt, to taste
6 tbsp **vegetable oil**
3 **medium-sized onions**, finely chopped
4 tbsp **tomato purée**
1 tsp **garam masala**
1 tsp **ginger**, cut into thin strips

Dijon Beef

Matt Watts

- Sauté the onion and garlic in the olive oil and butter, then add a little seasoning.
- As the onion starts to soften, add the mushrooms, then the steak. Cook for 2–3 minutes over a high heat, or until the steak is sealed or coloured.
- Add the paprika and Dijon mustard. Then add the brandy and ignite with a match to take the harsh edge off of the alcohol. Cook for a minute more.

- Add the lemon juice and double cream, and reduce by boiling it for a minute. Adjust the seasoning and serve immediately, with some braised or boiled white rice.

Serves 4

1 **large onion**, finely chopped
2–3 **garlic cloves**, crushed
50 ml (2 fl oz) **olive oil**
25 g (1 oz) **butter**
salt and **pepper**, to taste
150 g (5½ oz) **mushrooms**, sliced
700 g (1 lb 9 oz) **fillet steak**, cut into strips
1 tbsp **paprika**
2 tbsp **Dijon mustard**
4 tbsp **brandy**
1 tsp **lemon juice**
350 ml (12 fl oz) **double cream**

Left: Matt Watts on the beach at Newquay, with Ruby and Hamish.

Traditional Lancashire Hotpot

James Martin

- Preheat the oven to 170°C/340°F/gas mark 3–4, then trim the lamb of any excess fat and dry on some kitchen paper.
- Heat the groundnut oil and 5 g (⅛ oz) of the butter in a large frying pan until very hot, then brown the pieces of lamb two or three at a time. When fully cooked, transfer to a wide casserole dish, with 3.5-litre (6-pint) capacity.
- Brown the kidneys in the same way and tuck into the casserole dish among the lamb pieces.
- Adding a little more butter to the pan if necessary, fry the onions for about 10 minutes, or until brown at the edges. Stir in the flour to soak up the juice, then gradually add the hot water and Worcestershire sauce, stirring until smooth.
- Season with the sea salt and black pepper, and bring to simmering point. Pour over the meat in the casserole dish. Add the bay leaf and thyme sprigs, and cook in the oven for 90 minutes.
- Remove the meat mixture from the oven, adjusting the seasoning and removing the bay leaf. Then spoon into a casserole dish and arrange the potato slices on top in an overlapping pattern. Season the potatoes and add a few dots of butter over the surface.
- Cover with a tight-fitting lid or tin foil and cook in the oven for 30 minutes. Remove the lid during the last 15 minutes of cooking time, brush the potatoes with a little more butter and place under the grill for crisping. Alternatively, turn up the heat during the last 15 minutes of cooking time and remove the lid.
- Allow to cool, then reheat in the oven just before serving.

Serves 4–6

- 900 g (2 lb) **best end and middle neck of British lamb**, chopped into lamb chop-sized pieces
- 1 tbsp **groundnut** or other **flavourless oil**
- 25 g (1 oz) **unsalted butter**
- 4 **lamb's kidneys**, cored, skinned and chopped quite small
- 350 g (12 oz) **onions**, peeled and cut into 1-cm (½-in) wedges
- 1 tbsp **plain flour**
- 570 ml (1 pint) **hot water**
- ½ tsp **Worcestershire sauce**
- **sea salt** and **freshly ground black pepper**
- 1 **bay leaf**
- 2 **fresh thyme sprigs**
- 900 g (2 lb) **potatoes**, peeled and cut into 2-cm (¾-in) slices

Banoffi Pie

Matt Watts

- Submerge the condensed milk in a pan of boiling water for 3–3½ hours. Remember to keep the pan topped up with boiling water.
- Allow the container of boiled condensed milk, or toffee as it now is, to cool before opening. It is a good idea to boil a few containers at a time and store, still sealed, for future use.
- Meanwhile, crush the digestive biscuits in a blender, so they resemble crumbs. Then add the butter and mix thoroughly.
- Open the cooled toffee and blend with the bananas.
- Make individual banoffi pies by layering the biscuit mix and the toffee and banana mix in glasses or decorative bowls, and topping with the whipped cream. Alternatively, prepare a single pie in the same way, but using a 20-cm (8-in) cake tin.
- If you like, decorate the banoffi pie(s) with a little grated chocolate or some toasted almonds. Cool in the refrigerator and cut into wedges to serve.

Serves 4

1 x 250-ml (9-fl oz) container of **condensed milk**, unopened

1 packet of **digestive biscuits** (about 10 biscuits)

50 g (1¾ oz) **unsalted butter**, melted

3 **large bananas**, peeled and sliced

150 ml (5 fl oz) **whipped cream**

grated chocolate, to garnish (optional)

ground almonds, to garnish (optional)

Sticky Toffee Pudding with Butterscotch Sauce

Paul Rankin

- Preheat the oven to 180°C/350°F/gas mark 4. Then pour the boiling water over the dates and set aside to soak and cool.
- Sift the flour and bicarbonate of soda together and, in a separate bowl, add the vanilla and coffee essences to the milk.
- Cream the butter and sugar together until light and fluffy. Then slowly add the eggs, each time waiting until they have been fully incorporated before adding more.
- Alternately fold the flour and milk into the egg mixture. Lastly, pour in the dates. The result will be rather light and runnier than cake batter.
- Ladle the mixture into 6–8 oiled individual moulds and place on a baking sheet in the centre of the oven. Bake for about 30 minutes, or until the puddings are firm and starting to pull away from the sides of the moulds. Remove from the oven and turn out on to a wire rack to cool.
- To make the butterscotch sauce, put the butter into a medium-sized saucepan, over a medium-high heat. When it starts to bubble, add the brown sugar. Stir together for about 3 minutes, until the brown sugar has dissolved and the whole mass is foaming and bubbling.
- Carefully pour in the whipping cream, followed by the whiskey, and turn down the heat. Let it all come together and boil for another minute or two, then remove from the heat. Add the vanilla essence and allow to cool slightly.
- To serve, place the puddings on warm plates and ladle a generous spoonful of the sauce over each one. Dollops of whipped cream will top them off perfectly. If wrapped in clingfilm, the puddings keep well for a couple of days. They can be reheated in just a minute or two in the microwave or, covered in some of the sauce, in a medium-heat oven.

Serves 6–8

175 ml (6 fl oz) **boiling water**
200 g (9 oz) **fresh dates**, stoned and finely chopped
175 g (6 oz) **self-raising flour**
1 tsp **bicarbonate of soda**
1 tsp **vanilla essence**
1 tbsp **coffee essence**
100 ml (3½ fl oz) **whole milk**
85 g (3 oz) **unsalted butter**
140 g (5 oz) **sugar**
2 **eggs**, beaten just to break the yolks
vegetable oil, for greasing
whipped cream, to serve

For the butterscotch sauce:
3 tbsp **unsalted butter**
8 tbsp **light golden brown sugar**
200 ml (7 fl oz) **whipping cream**
200 ml (7 fl oz) **Irish whiskey**
1 tbsp **vanilla essence**

Simple Chocolate Truffle Cake

Matt Watts

- To make the chocolate sponge, whisk together the caster sugar and eggs in a bowl set over hot water until the mixture thickens and forms tracks or ribbons as you draw the whisk through it. Next, fold in the cornflour and cocoa powder.
- Pour on to a baking dish lined with baking paper and spread thinly. Bake for about 5 minutes in the oven at 230°C/450°F/ gas mark 8.
- Meanwhile, line 4 x 7.5 x 5-cm (3 x 2-in) moulds or cups with cling film. Lightly whip the cream and melt the chocolate in a bowl set over a pan of simmering water.
- Set the chocolate aside to cool slightly before folding into the whipping cream with a whisk. Fill the moulds with the mousse mixture. In a separate bowl, mix together the orange juice and Grand Marnier.
- Cut the chocolate sponge into disks to place on top of the moulds. Brush with the orange juice and Grand Marnier mixture, place on top of the moulds, then place the moulds in the refrigerator to set and cool.
- Unmould the truffle cakes by swiftly turning the moulds upside down. Dust the cakes with the cocoa powder and serve.

Serves 4

For the chocolate sponge:
100 g (3½ oz) **caster sugar**
4 **eggs**
50 g (1¾ oz) **cornflour**
50 g (1¾ oz) **cocoa powder**

300 ml (10 fl oz) **whipping cream**
200 g (7 oz) **dark** or **plain chocolate**
50 ml (2 fl oz) **orange juice**
50 ml (2 fl oz) **Grand Marnier cocoa powde**r, for dusting

White Chocolate, Whisky and Croissant Pudding

James Martin

- Preheat the oven to 200°C/400°F/gas mark 6. Pour the milk and double cream into a pan, add the vanilla pod and gradually bring to the boil.
- Gently mix together the eggs, egg-yolks and caster sugar in a separate bowl.
- Meanwhile, slice the croissants and place in an ovenproof dish, slightly overlapping the pieces. Sprinkle with the sultanas and pour over the butter.
- Remove the cream mixture from the heat when it starts to boil and add the eggs and white chocolate. Stir well, then set aside to allow the chocolate to melt, stirring occasionally.
- Add the whisky, then, using a sieve, strain over the croissants. Cover the dish with foil and bake in the oven for 15–20 minutes, or until almost set.
- Remove from the oven, coat the top of the croissants with the apricot jam, and dust with the icing sugar. Caramelise the topping using a very hot grill or, if you have one, a blowtorch. This is best served at room temperature, with a spoonful of good-quality vanilla ice cream.

Serves 4

500 ml (18 fl oz) **whole milk**
500 ml (18 fl oz) **double cream**
1 **vanilla pod**
3 **eggs**
5 **egg-yolks**
200 g (7 oz) **caster sugar**
4 **large croissants**
25 g (1 oz) **sultanas**
25 g (1 oz) **unsalted butter**, melted
175 g (6 oz) **white chocolate**, grated
3 tbsp **whisky**
55 g (2 oz) **apricot jam**
icing sugar, for dusting
vanilla ice cream, to taste

Vanilla Panna Cottas with Summer Fruits

Allan and Eileen Donald

- Soften the gelatine leaves for a few minutes in a tub of cold water. Meanwhile, combine the milk, double cream and vanilla pod and seeds in a pan, and bring to the boil. Remove from the heat and whisk in the caster sugar and softened gelatine.

- Set the pan over a bowl of ice and whisk until the ingredients start to set. Remove the vanilla pod, then pass the mixture through a sieve into small pudding moulds and refrigerate for 1–2 hours.

- To prepare the consommé, place the strawberries in a heatproof bowl and cover with cling film. Set the bowl over a pan of simmering water for 40 minutes. When most of the colour has come out of the strawberries, pass through a fine sieve. While the juice is still warm, stir in the caster sugar until dissolved.

- To serve, unmould the panna cottas and place in the centre of a bowl. Scatter over the berries, then top with the consommé.

Serves 10

For the panna cottas:
3 **gelatine leaves**
300 ml (10 fl oz) **whole milk**
700 ml (1¼ pint) **double cream**
1 **vanilla pod** (seeds scraped out and reserved)
100 g (3½ oz) **caster sugar**
strawberries, **raspberries** and **blueberries**, to garnish

For the strawberry consommé:
500 g (1 lb 2 oz) **fresh strawberries**, hulled and quartered
70 g (2½ oz) **caster sugar**

Lemon Curd Syllabub

James Martin

- Crumble a biscuit each into the bottom of 4 sundae dishes or glasses and moisten with half of the white wine.
- Begin whipping the double cream with the icing sugar and, when it forms soft peaks, fold in the remaining wine and swirl in the lemon curd, leaving a marbling of yellow through the cream.
- Spoon the mixture into the dishes and scatter with the flaked almonds. Garnish with the mint sprigs and serve.

Serves 4

4 **lemon** or **plain shortbread biscuits**
100 ml (3½ fl oz) **white wine**
250 ml (9 oz) **double cream**
4 tbsp **icing sugar**
8 tbsp **lemon curd**
2 tbsp **flaked almonds**, toasted
2 **fresh mint sprigs**

Left: Fudge Martin keeps watch.

Chocolate Tarts

John Burton Race

- To make the sweet pastry, beat together the butter and icing sugar until light and fluffy. Add the eggs one at a time and beat into the butter until smooth. Add the flour and mix to a smooth paste. With a spatula, turn out the pastry on to a lightly floured surface and mould to form a ball.

- Cover the pastry in cling film and place in the refrigerator to rest for at least 2 hours. When ready, roll it out and line 10 x 7-cm (2¾-in) ring moulds. Carefully place the moulds on a baking tray and put in the refrigerator to rest.

- To make the chocolate filling, chop half of the bitter chocolate into small pieces. Place in a heatproof bowl over a pan half filled with hot water and stir until melted. Pour the chocolate into an ice-cube tray, half filling 10 compartments, and place the tray in the freezer to set. Chop up the remaining bitter chocolate and butter, and melt in the same way.

- Put the egg-whites into a stainless-steel mixing bowl and whisk until they form stiff peaks. Add the caster sugar at the end to form a smooth meringue. Next, stir the egg-yolk into the chocolate mixture. Gently fold the egg-white mixture in, too. Remove the pastry moulds from the refrigerator and half fill with the chocolate mousse.

- Take the chocolate cubes out of the freezer and turn out. Put one cube into the centre of each mould. Spoon a little more chocolate mousse over the cubes. Place the tarts into the freezer until set, about 3 hours. Preheat the oven to 180°C/350°F/gas mark 4. Remove the tarts from the freezer and bake in the oven for about 12 minutes. Using a fish slice, remove from the oven one by one and place in the centre of some dessert plates. Carefully remove the ring moulds.

Serves 10

For the sweet pastry:
300 g (10½ oz) **unsalted butter**
115 g (4 oz) **icing sugar**
2 **eggs**
500 g (1 lb 2 oz) **plain flour**

250 g (9 oz) **bitter chocolate** (70% cocoa solids)
35 g (1¼ oz) **unsalted butter**
4 **egg-whites**
30 g (1¼ oz) **caster sugar**
1 **egg-yolk**

Below: John Burton Race with his children and Fendi.

Petsavers' Projects

In 2004, Petsavers funded the first scholarship post dedicated to rabbit medicine and surgery. This three-year position will increase our understanding of this popular pet.

Cardhu, a much-loved cat with signs of senility, prompted his owner Dr Danielle Gunn-Moore to investigate, with the help of Petsavers funding, changes in the brains of old cats.

Marcus caught infectious hepatitis just before he was fully vaccinated. Petsavers funds the training of specialist vets so that such ill patients will have the best possible chance of recovery.

Josh suffered from diabetes before developing kidney failure and hyperthyroidism. Petsavers has funded studies into the best ways of managing these conditions.

Skipper, a minature schnauzer, suffered with bladder stones. The cause of the stones was not known until Petsavers-funded clinical studies helped to identify the problem. Skipper is now doing well and is a much happier little dog.

Petsavers funding has enabled identification of the tick that transmits disease in captive birds, such as this peregrine falcon.

Hyperthyroidism, or over-active thyroids, is a common affliction among older cats. Petsavers is funding a study into how this condition develops.

Petsavers has funded veterinary studies that aim to improve the management of diabetes in dogs such as Libby. The studies' findings will allow ill patients to spend less time in the veterinary hospital and more time at home.

Petsavers has funded a project to improve testing for auto-immune blood diseases in cats.

Megan became seriously ill with a lungworm infection known as angiostrongylosis. She was diagnosed promptly and made a full recovery, thanks to Petsavers.

One Petsavers-funded project looked at the high incidence of worms in pets kept at rescue centres. Its findings are expected to improve the well-being of dogs such as Milly.

Petsavers has funded a number of studies into the diseases that afflict aviary birds in the UK, such as this barn owl.

Cavalier King Charles spaniels, such as Chloë, can suffer from painful inflammation of the pancreas. An ongoing Petsavers-funded project is helping to increase our understanding of the disease.

Petsavers is helping to make the diagnosis of middle ear disease in dogs easier, more reliable and more affordable for all.

Petsavers is improving vets' ability to investigate the causes of anaemia in cats.

About Petsavers

Our pets provide us with love and companionship during our lives. We take care of them and seek expert help and advice from our vet when they fall ill or are injured – and expect our animals to be treated and to recover from their illnesses or injuries. However, there are still many diseases, like many human conditions, that we do not fully understand.

The charity Petsavers aims to change this by funding studies into the illnesses affecting our pets, as well as training programmes designed to advance the skills of vets.

Our ultimate aim is to improve the health of the nation's pets by relieving the distress and pain caused by illnesses for which we currently have no effective treatments.

Petsavers was started in 1974 by a group of veterinary surgeons who realised that despite our reputation as a nation of animal lovers, no organisation existed to specifically fund veterinary studies into diseases that affect pets. Since then, Petsavers has given over £1.7 million towards numerous studies that do not involve the use of experimental animals.

Petsavers awards grants via a committee consisting of expert veterinary surgeons. Some grants are used to fund training programmes (scholarships), which allow individual veterinary surgeons to develop an area of expertise in patient care. Other grants are awarded to fund studies into illnesses affecting pets. These help veterinary surgeons to understand more about the mechanisms of disease and to develop better treatment, allowing their patients to live longer and healthier lives.

Petsavers has already had success in gaining a better understanding of many common ailments such as kidney failure in cats, arthritis in dogs, diabetes, cancer, heart disease and skin complaints. However, sources of funding for veterinary studies are scarce and the need for Petsavers has become even greater.

HOW YOU CAN SUPPORT PETSAVERS

You can help to support the vital work of Petsavers in many ways. Please let us know how you would like to help us by simply ticking one or more of the boxes and completing your name and address overleaf. Photocopy or tear out this slip and send it to:

Petsavers, c/o BSAVA, Woodrow House, 1 Telford Way, Waterwells Business Park, Quedgeley, Gloucester GL2 2AB

☐ Making a donation

Please complete this form with your details and send it to Petsavers with your contribution.

☐ Making a long-standing commitment to Petsavers

By making a donation on a regular basis through a standing order, you will allow Petsavers to plan for the future and to make commitments to further research projects.

☐ Nominating Petsavers as a beneficiary in your will

We will send you a free Petsavers' booklet with further information on the benefits of making a will and how to leave a donation to Petsavers in your will.

☐ Taking part in a sponsored event

Whatever your ambition, there is bound to be an event for you. We can provide a list of possibilities and fund-raising support.

☐ Organising your own fund-raising event

We will provide you with a fund-raising pack full of ideas and advice.

☐ Purchasing and/or selling Petsavers' Christmas cards.

Each year we offer a new selection of cards.

Petsavers, BSAVA, Woodrow House, 1 Telford Way, Waterwells Business Park, Quedgeley, Gloucester GL2 2AB

T: 01452 726 723/706, F: 01452 726 701
E-mail: info@petsavers.org.uk
Website: www.petsavers.org.uk

I would like to support Petsavers by making a donation of £ _____

Name:
_____

Address:
_____

_____

_____

Postcode: _____

E-mail:
_____

Telephone no:
_____

I enclose a cheque/postal order [made payable to **Petsavers**] or please debit my Mastercard, Visa or Switch/Maestro Card [please delete as appropriate]
Card No: _____/_____/_____/_____

Expiry Date: ___/___ **Valid From:** ___/___

Card Holder: _____

Issue No. (Switch/Maestro): ____

You can make this gift go even further if you are a UK taxpayer. For every £10 you give, Petsavers can claim an extra £2.80 from the Inland Revenue at no extra cost to you.

☐ Simply tick this box to confirm that you would like Petsavers to reclaim tax on this and all future donations.

To qualify for gift aid, you must pay income or capital gains tax at least equivalent to the amount we will claim in the tax year.

Chefs' Details

Irish celebrity chef **Darina Allen** is the woman behind Ballymaloe Cookery School, Shanagarry, Midleton, Co Cork, Ireland. www.cookingisfun.ie

K.K. Anand is head chef of The Mint Leaf, Suffolk Place, Haymarket, London, SWIY 4HX. www.mintleafrestaurant.com

Celebrity chef **John Burton Race** owns The New Angel restaurant, 2 South Embankment, Dartmouth, Devon TQ6 9BH. www.thenewangel.co.uk

Stuart Conibear is head chef of Graffiti restaurant at Hotel Felix, Whitehouse Lane, Huntingdon Road, Cambridge, CB3 0LX. www.hotelfelix.co.uk

Allan Donald holds a Michelin star and is the recipient of numerous honours, including the Scottish Chefs Association's Scottish Chef of the Year award 2004. He and his wife, **Eileen,** are based at Ballachulish House, Ballachulish, Argyll PH49 4JX. www.ballachulishhouse.com

Celebrity chef **Anton Edelmann** is chef patron of Allium restaurant, Dolphin Square, Chichester Street, London SW1V 3LX. www.allium.co.uk

Ainsley Harriott is a celebrity chef and author. www.jeremyhicks.com/ainsleyharriott/biog.htm

Nigel Haworth is co-owner and head chef of restaurant and hotel Northcote Manor, Northcote Road, Langho, Blackburn, Lancashire BB6 8BE. www.northcotemanor.com

Celebrity chef and owner of 10 restaurants in the north-west of England, **Paul Heathcote** is the recipient of Egon Ronay's Chef of the Year honour and holds two Michelin stars. www.heathcotes.co.uk

Author and recipient of several accolades, including the AA Chefs' Chef of the Year award 2003, **Shaun Hill** was owner and head chef of Shropshire's respected The Merchant House restaurant until February 2005.

Ben McKellar owns two Brighton restaurants: Gingerman at Norfolk Square, 21A Norfolk Square, BN1 2PD, where he is also head chef, and Gingerman at Drakes, Drakes Hotel, 44 Marine Parade BN2 1PE. www.gingermanrestaurants.com

Celebrity chef **James Martin** is co-owner of bespoke kitchen manufacturer Underwood & James and Cadogan & James deli and café, 31A The Square, Winchester, www.jamesmartinchef.co.uk

Morgan Meunier is owner and head chef of Morgan M, 489 Liverpool Road, London N7 8NS, short-listed for French Restaurant of the Year 2004 and 2005 in the Tio Pepe ITV London Restaurant Awards. www.morganm.com

Alan Monks is owner of caterer Stravaigin's, Two Little Ducks Cottage, Church Road, Lymm, Cheshire WA13 0QQ. www.stravaigins-caterers-lymm.co.uk

Nathan Outlaw is head chef of St Ervan Manor, St Ervan, Padstow, Cornwall, PL27 7TA. www.stervanmanor.co.uk

Raymond Patterson is owner and head chef of Patterson's Restaurant, 4 Mill St, Mayfair, London W1S 2AX. www.pattersonsrestaurant.com

Irish celebrity chef **Paul Rankin** is proprietor of Cayenne Restaurant, Ascot House, Shaftsbury Square, Belfast BT2 7DB. www.cayennerestaurant.com

Celebrity chef **Delia Smith** is the author of numerous cookbooks and director of Norwich City Football Club. www.deliaonline.co.uk

Celebrity chef **Rick Stein** owns the Seafood Restaurant, Riverside, Padstow, Cornwall, PL28 8BY. www.rickstein.com

Chris and **James Tanner** own Tanners Restaurant, Prysten House, Finewell Street, Plymouth, Devon PL1 2AE. www.tannersrestaurant.com

Jake Watkins is owner and head chef of JSW restaurant, 1 Heath Road, Petersfield, Hampshire GU31 4JE.

Matthew Watts is head chef of The Cocked Hat Restaurant, Rugby Road, Binley Woods, Coventry CV3 2AY.

Celebrity chef **Antony Worrall Thompson** owns Notting Grill, 123A Clarendon Road, London W11 4JG; the Kew Grill, 10B Kew Green, Richmond, Surrey TW9 3BH; and The Angel Coaching Inn and Grill, High Street, Heytesbury, Nr Warminster, Wiltshire BA12 0ED. www.awtonline.co.uk

Recipe Credits

Butter-Bean, Chorizo and Cabbage Soup; Tomato Fondue; Winter Vegetable and Bean Soup with Spicy Sausage (recipe reproduced by permission from *A Year at Ballymaloe Cookery School*, published by Kyle Cathie) © Darina Allen

Black Pepper Prawns (Jheenga Kali Mirch), Pan-Grilled Lamb Cutlets (Masala Champey) © K. K. Anand

Chocolate Tarts © John Burton Race

Breast of Duckling with Fresh Berries and Apple Mash, Melon Gazpacho Iced © Stuart Conibear

Linguine with Loch Linnhe Langoustines, Vanilla Panna Cottas with Summer Fruits © Allan and Eileen Donald

Fried Noodles with Teriyaki Salmon, Roasted Figs with Goat's Cheese, Spicy Sausage with Pasta and Vegetables © Anton Edelmann

Chargrilled Red Mullet with Spicy, Sunny Savoy Cabbage; Peppered Chicken Salad © Ainsley Harriott

Twice-Baked Lancashire Soufflés © Nigel Haworth

Potato, Garlic and Parsley Pie © Paul Heathcote

Grilled Haddock with Mustard, Lentil and Celeriac Sauce © Shaun Hill

Roasted Corn-Fed Chicken with New Season Garlic © Ben McKellar

Chicken Tikka Masala; Green Pea and Smoked Salmon

Risotto; Lemon Curd Syllabub; Parma Ham with Purple Figs and Minted Yoghurt; Penne with Pancetta and Flat-Leaf Parsley; Traditional Lancashire Hotpot; White Chocolate, Whisky and Croissant Pudding © James Martin

Steamed Wild Sea Bass with Pastis and Saffron Sauce © Morgan Meunier

Spicy, Fried Fish Cakes (Tod Man Pla) © Alan Monks

Cornish Dived Scallops with Braised Oxtail © Nathan Outlaw

Poussin with Asparagus © Raymond Patterson

Sticky Toffee Pudding with Butterscotch Sauce © Paul Rankin

Roasted Salmon Fillets with a

Pecorino and Pesto Topping © Delia Smith 1999 (recipe reproduced by permission from *Delia's How to Cook Book Two*, published by BBC Worldwide)

Salt and Pepper Prawns, Stir-Fried Salt and Pepper Squid © Rick Stein

Salad of Spring Lamb Niçoise-Style with Egg Dressing, Warm Salad of Honey and Mustard Glazed Chicken © Chris and James Tanner

Confit of Wild Salmon with Watercress Risotto © Jake Watkins

Banoffi Pie, Dijon Beef, Roasted Lamb Loin with Chorizo, Simple Chocolate Truffle Cake © Matt Watts

Cheese and Bacon Soufflé © Antony Worrall Thompson

Photography Credits

1 left James Martin, middle Rick Stein, right K. K. Anand; 3 left and right Chris and James Tanner; 9 Rick Stein; 11 M. Martin; 12 Alan Monks; 13 Alan Monks; 15 Darina Allen; 17 Darina Allen (photograph reproduced by permission from *A Year at Ballymaloe Cookery School*, published by Kyle Cathie); 18 Antony Worrall Thompson; 21 Nigel Haworth; 23 Ainsley Harriott; 25 Delia Smith 1999 (photograph reproduced by permission from *Delia's How to Cook Book Two*, published by BBC Worldwide); 26 K. K. Anand; 27 K. K. Anand; 29 Morgan Meunier; 30 M. Martin; 31 M. Martin; 32 Anton Edelmann; 33 M. Martin; 35 Rick Stein; 37 James Martin; 39 M. Martin; 40 Allan and Eileen Donald; 42 Chris and James Tanner; 43 Chris and James Tanner; 45 Stuart Conibear; 47 Ainsley Harriott; 49 James Martin; 50 Chris and James Tanner; 51 Chris and James Tanner; 53 M. Martin; 54 K. K. Anand; 55 Matt Watts; 57 Jean Cazals (photograph reproduced by permission from *Great British Dinners*, published by Mitchell Beazley); 59 M. Martin; 61 Paul Rankin; 63 M. Martin; 65 photograph reproduced by permission from Mitchell Beazley; 67 Roy Summers (photograph reproduced by permission from *Scottish Field* magazine); 68 James Martin; 69 John Burton Race; 70 left A. Meredith, middle Danielle Gunn-Moore, right Ian Ramsey; 71 left and middle Ian Ramsey, right John Chitty; 72 left Sean Callanan, middle L. Davison, right M. Martin; 73 left and middle M. Martin, right Neil Forbes; 74 left M. Martin, middle Ross Doust, right S. Tasker; 80 Toby Gemmell; Jacket: front left James Martin; front middle Antony Worrall Thompson; front right Ainsley Harriott; front flap Chris and James Tanner; spine Roy Summers (photograph reproduced by permission from *Scottish Field* magazine); back left Jean Cazals (photograph reproduced by permission from *Great British Dinners*, published by Mitchell Beazley); back right photograph reproduced by permission from Mitchell Beazley

Index